Other Titles by Ronald Reed:

Tallmadge Hill (2013)

Derby Downs

The 1936 and 1937 All-American Soap Box Derbies

Ronald Reed

Derby Downs
The 1936 And 1937 All-American Soap Box Derbies

iUniverse books may be ordered through booksellers or by contacting:

iUniverse LLC
1663 Liberty Drive
Bloomington, IN 47403
www.iuniverse.com
1-800-Authors (1-800-288-4677)

ISBN: 978-1-4917-4552-6 (sc)
ISBN: 978-1-4917-4551-9 (e)

Library of Congress Control Number: 2014916237

Printed in the United States of America.

iUniverse rev. date: 09/23/2014

CONTENTS

To Valerie Sue Carlton, my "precious jewel of a daughter," who combines working a full-time job with being a homemaker and a soccer mom, chasing two active sons, and still making time for Dad.

PREFACE

There's an old saying that goes, "There are two things that people think they can do better than the ones doing them. One is writing songs, and the other is umpiring baseball." I would like to add a third: winning at Soap Box Derby racing.

Being from the Akron area, I grew up with the Soap Box Derby. Everyone was either building a car or knew someone who was. Everyone, that is, except me. I couldn't build anything. I was the guy who, along with my buddy Chuck Pope, constructed a doghouse for my pet Henry and then couldn't get it out of the basement. Okay, so maybe I would never be the All-American Soap Box Derby champion and never ride in a new Chevy convertible waving to a cheering crowd of fifty thousand people. But I could still attend the race every year and have a ball. And I did! My introduction to the derby, at age seven, took place in 1949 when my uncle Bob took me and my dad to the race. "This is the one we are rooting for," my father told me as the Akron champ, Fred Derks, won his first heat by a large margin. I was hooked. Even at seven I knew that when I saw "Akron Beacon Journal" painted on the side of a racer, it was the one I wanted to cheer on to the championship heat.

There have been seventy-seven All-American races, and I have seen sixty-four of them—not bad, considering that the first eight took place before I was born. Throughout my teen years, I purchased photos of each year's final heat from the *Akron Beacon Journal*. The next step was compiling a scrapbook and enlarging my collection. Soon, one scrapbook was not large enough to accommodate all that I had. One scrapbook became two, then three, four, and five, until now—with the advent of the masters, kit, stock, and superstock divisions, plus the addition of the rally program—the total has swelled to 154 books. When a former contestant or parent requests a photo from a time that he or she raced, I simply go to my bookcase and extract, say, the junior division book for 1981 and copy whatever photo is wanted. The idea of writing a book on the history of the derby has always been in the back of my mind, but I soon realized that covering all seventy-six years with their rule changes, local races, celebrities, human-interest stories, and all the events of the race days would require a three-thousand-page book. The market for a book of that magnitude is, to say the least, limited. And with my hunt-and-peck typing skills, it would probably take me about thirty years to write it. The answer seemed to be separating the story into eras that could be told in installments. The first installment, entitled *Tallmadge Hill*, was published in 2013 and dealt with the inception of the derby in 1933 as a city race in Dayton, Ohio, and how the originator, Myron Scott, turned his brainchild into a national event in 1934 and moved it to Akron in 1935. This second installment, called *Derby Downs*, covers the events of 1936, with the derby finding a permanent home, and continues through the 1937 race. To the best of my knowledge, these are the events of those two years exactly the way they occurred.

Most of the photos contained herein are taken from Chevrolet's files in Detroit, the archives of the *Akron Beacon Journal*, various libraries across the country, and the private collections of some great derby fans. A few are microfilm reproductions and excerpts from the 1936 derby film produced by Chevrolet. They are not of the best quality, but I hope this does not detract from your enjoyment of the story.

ACKNOWLEDGMENTS

I wish to thank McCreary Photography, a former company in Akron, for the use of many race-day photos. Another supplier of pictures was the All-American Soap Box Derby itself, along with Jeff Iula and Tex Finsterwald, who supplied photos from their private collections. General Motors Photographic Handy (Jam) provided additional material. Of course, the Akron Summit County Public Library, along with many other libraries across the nation, provided microfilm information. I don't want to leave out my uncle Bob Reed, the one who initially got me interested in the derby.

My granddaughter Teghan Reed, who did all of my scanning, and her mother, Leslie, who, as usual, corrected my mistakes, deserve most of the credit.

INTRODUCTION

What Is the Soap Box Derby?

The initial race, created by Myron Scott, originated in 1933 in Dayton, Ohio. Scott had witnessed several boys racing their homemade cars on a neighborhood hill. This sparked an idea; Scott reported and photographed for an article to appear in the *Dayton Daily News*. He asked the boys to return in two weeks and bring some friends. The race was run, and a loving cup was presented to the winner. Scott saw the potential and immediately began planning a citywide race with the *Dayton Daily News* as the sponsor.

On August 19, 1933, a total of 362 young lads participated in the contest to name the fastest boy in Dayton. Randall Custer prevailed in his three-wheeled creation, which featured a gas pipe instead of a steering wheel. The enthusiasm shown by the thousands of spectators witnessing these races convinced Scott that this competition had the potential to be something special.

Plans were made to make his race an annual, national event. He realized the importance of having a national sponsor and pitched the idea to the Chevrolet Motor Company in Detroit. The automobile manufacturer embraced the idea and enlisted its advertising firm, the Campbell-Ewald Company, to promote the event.

After much deliberation, Scott decided on the name Soap Box Derby, although there is no documentation that there was ever a racer built from a soapbox. He also designed a logo featuring a car that competed in the 1933 race. This logo was used by the derby for more than thirty years (see front cover). Next, he enlisted newspapers across the country to sponsor the local races in cooperation with Chevrolet. This proved a brilliant idea; the press was the perfect venue to convey times, dates, and rule requirements to the boys.

The 1934 All-American race featured thirty-four city winners from across the country. Bob Turner of Muncie, Indiana, was crowned the winner. The All-American Soap Box Derby moved to Akron, Ohio, in 1935, where it has remained. The first race in Akron was held on Tallmadge Hill and was won by Maurice Bale of Anderson, Indiana. The next year, 1936, brought the construction of Derby Downs, the permanent home of the All-American race.

PART 1

PROLOGUE

The World in 1936

In 1936, the Depression was still the nation's biggest problem. The Works Progress Administration (WPA) had been created by the federal government to put people back to work on various construction projects. One of these projects was Derby Downs in Akron.

Americans saw unemployment decrease from 20.1 percent in 1935 to 16.9 percent in 1936. Everyone waited with cautious optimism. Perhaps there was a light at the end of the tunnel.

In international news, King Edward of England abdicated the throne to marry an American divorcée, saying he could not carry on his duties without the help of "the woman I love." President Roosevelt, despite his detractors, won a landslide victory over Republican presidential hopeful Alf Landon. In national news, Alvin "Creepy" Karpis, the last of the "Public Enemies," was arrested in New Orleans.

On radio, FDR's fireside chats kept the public informed of the latest government events in a way it could understand. On the lighter side, Edgar Bergen's alter egos Charlie McCarthy and Mortimer Snerd kept the kiddies entertained, as did the newest crime fighter, the Green Hornet. In the comics, Felix the Cat appeared on the scene to delight youngsters all over America.

In the world of sports, Ohio State sprinter Jesse Owens took the Berlin Summer Olympics by storm, much to the chagrin of Adolf Hitler. In baseball, "Rapid Robert" Feller made his debut with the Cleveland Indians, as did "Joltin' Joe" DiMaggio with the New York Yankees. The Baseball Hall of Fame was created with five members voted into the inaugural class: Babe Ruth, Honus Wagner, Ty Cobb, Christy Mathewson, and Walter Johnson. Minnesota's Golden Gophers were the kings of college football, and in boxing Max Schmeling knocked out Joe Louis.

In Hollywood, the Oscar for best picture went to *The Great Ziegfeld.* Other notable flicks were *Mr. Deeds Goes to Town, My Man Godfrey, Rose Marie,* and *The Petrified Forest.*

Everyone was singing "A Fine Romance," "I'm an Old Cowhand," "Pennies from Heaven," "I've Got You Under My Skin," "Stardust," "These Foolish Things," and "I'm Getting Sentimental Over You."

Notables born in 1936 include Robert Redford, Michael Landon, Burt Reynolds, Mary Tyler Moore, Dean Stockwell, Buddy Holly, Wilt Chamberlain, and Alan Alda.

LEADING UP TO THE RACE

Chevrolet operated three traveling field offices. Chevy staff members assisted local race personnel with their city races and promoted the All-American Derby at every stop.

The field offices

The Rules

A more formal rule book was introduced for 1936 with twenty basic rules, illustrated with photos. There were sections with construction hints, suggested styles, and instructions on how to construct steering assemblies and brakes. This thirty-two page booklet was most helpful. The rule changes for 1936 were significant but not sweeping. Car and boy together could not weigh more than 250 pounds, and the car could not cost more than ten dollars to construct. The axle and steering rods could be taken to a machine shop to be cut to size, but no other work could be done there. Wheel sizes were standardized, so the twenty-inch bicycle wheels, which were so popular in 1935, were out. Edwin T. Hamilton, managing editor of *Model Craftsman* magazine, was added to the National Technical Committee. He edited a section of the new rule book entitled "Suggestions to Builders" that featured construction sketches of different types of cars that were then popular among boy builders.

The 1936 rule book

Tickets

With the construction of grandstands, tickets could be printed with assigned seating. The 1936 tickets were a handsome creation featuring a photo of the final heat of 1935.

The 1936 ticket

Programs

Another first for 1936 was the introduction of programs. While this first effort had its shortcomings, it did provide some useful information. A simple fold-out card, it listed the awards, city sponsors, and the first-round lineup.

The program front

The Track

The All-American Soap Box Derby had no permanent home prior to 1936. It had been held on city streets, both in Dayton in 1934 and Akron in 1935. The main factor in moving the race to Akron was the promise of a special racing facility to be ready by August 1936. This would be the third location in three years, but race officials hoped that if the venue was good enough, it might become that much-needed permanent home. A site was selected near the Akron Airport, southeast of downtown Akron and only one thousand yards east of the hangar where the airships *Akron* and *Macon* were constructed. The track was to run south to north. The hill was already there, so the next objective was to establish the proper length and grade. Derby originator Myron Scott, airport manager Bain "Shorty" Fulton, and *Akron Beacon Journal* Sports Editor Jim Schlemmer supervised every step of the construction. Thousands of yards of dirt were moved by boy-powered wheelbarrows to achieve the needed grade.

Next came the paving. The width of the track was set at thirty feet—three lanes of ten feet each. The length was 1,600 feet, with the level area (topside) before the starting line to serve as the staging area and another 300 feet past the finish line to enable safe stopping. Once the concrete ribbon was poured and firm, the actual racing distance needed to be determined, keeping the safety of the boys in mind. Aiding in this effort was the 1935 Akron champion and third-place winner in the All-American race, Loney Kline, who drove his racer down the hill countless times while race officials timed his speed to determine the exact spots for the starting and finish lines. All the while, construction crews were working to build grandstands near the finish line and bleachers along the rest of the track. The other major project was the construction of a wooden bridge spanning the finish line to house the media, communications, and photography people.

Newly constructed Derby Downs; note Heisman Lodge at left

The bridge, the nerve center of the facility

Heisman Lodge

Eighty yards to the east of the track was a building known as the Heisman Lodge. Originally built as a shelter for the skiers who populated the nearby hillsides, it was named after John Heisman, the legendary football coach after whom the famous trophy is named. Heisman coached at Buchtel College, which was later renamed the University of Akron. The Toledo Scale Company handled the weighing in of each car and driver to make sure that all 116 contestants were under the weight limit. The B. F. Goodrich Company installed a five-bay service pit in the topside area. It was manned by qualified Goodrich employees, who performed adjustments on the racers and handled any repairs needed due to collisions.

The service pits

Meanwhile, sixty-seven cities were denied local race franchises because Akron just didn't have the hotel facilities to handle the families of that many champs. Some of the notable cities denied were Fargo, North Dakota; Salt Lake City, Utah; Rittman, Ohio; and Charleston, South Carolina. Stories appeared daily in the *Akron Beacon Journal* about local races in other cities. Over 147,000 boys raced throughout the nation. The first-ever foreign champ arrived in Akron several days before the race. Pretoria, South Africa, had held a local race and crowned its champ, sixteen year-old Norman Neumann. The construction of his car was rumored to have cost more than a hundred dollars, although this could not be confirmed.

Pretoria's Norman Neumann

RACE DAY

///

Mother Nature cooperated beautifully, providing a perfect day for racing. The race time temperature was eighty degrees, and a slight breeze blew west to east across the track. The prerace parade began as scheduled. Down the hill came the color guard, bands, guests, and 116 champs, led by Norman Neumann. At the conclusion, a band played the "Star-Spangled Banner" as the Goodyear blimp hovered overhead. With everything in place, it was time to begin the competition.

Celebrities

Eddie Rickenbacker, the World War I flying ace and owner of the Indianapolis Motor Speedway, was back in Akron for the derby. Besides visiting with the champs, his main function was to award the Indianapolis Motor Speedway trophy to the boy who recorded the fastest winning time of the day. A race car driver at twenty-two, he joined the army at the outbreak of WWI and became the ace of the Army Air Corps with twenty-six kills. He purchased the Indianapolis Speedway in 1927 and operated it until 1945. He also bought Eastern Airlines in 1938. He passed away while in Zurich, Switzerland, in 1973.

Known as the fastest man on water, Gar Wood (1880–1971) was in town to take part in the festivities. Wood was the first man to travel over one hundred miles per hour on water. A designer of speedboats and pleasure crafts, he pioneered speedboat racing in the United States and abroad.

Ted Husing (1901–1962) was a legendary sports announcer. He described sports events in such detail that listeners would swear they could picture the events as they unfolded. His smooth, resonant voice enthralled millions. Rated number twelve of the top fifty sportscasters of all time, he was largely responsible for play-by-play as we know it today. He is also the man responsible for football referees' giving signals to the press box to explain the various penalties. This was Husing's first Soap Box Derby, but it would not be his last.

NBC broadcasting great Graham McNamee (1888–1942) had been hit the previous year by the runaway car of Oklahoma City's Paul Brown, and it looked as though McNamee wouldn't be able to attend the race due to scheduling conflicts. But when McNamee heard that Brown had won again, he issued the following statement: "My work has brought me face to face with dangers of all kinds and I have escaped injury from everything but a home-made Soap Box Derby car. If I don't go back to Akron to broadcast this year's Soap Box Derby the nation will think I cannot take it." He juggled his schedule and once again was in Akron for the race. In 1984, McNamee was inducted into the American Sportscasters Association Hall of Fame's inaugural class, which included legends Red Barber, Don Dunphy, Ted Husing, and Bill Stern. He was also inducted into the National Radio Hall of Fame in 2011. Among his notable broadcasts was that announcing the return of Lindburgh to New York after his historic flight, as well as the broadcast of the 1926 World Series.

Tom Manning (1899–1969), a well-known sportscaster in Ohio, aired play-by-play broadcasts for both the Cleveland Indians and the Ohio State Buckeyes. He retired in 1967.

Veteran race driver and three-time Indianapolis 500 runner-up Harry Hartz (1896–1974) served as race referee and flagman at the finish line, as he had in 1935. He also took part in welcoming the champs to Akron. A tireless worker, he made sure things ran smoothly, attending many of the local races. Hartz raced in the Indianapolis 500 six times, placing second three times and fourth twice. He was inducted into the National Sprint Car Hall of Fame in 1998.

"Wild Bill" Cummings (1906–1939), the 1934 Indianapolis 500 winner, was attending the derby for the third straight year. He spent countless hours with the champs discussing speed and the importance of good and safe driving. The boys listened intently to the man who had proven he knew what he was talking about.

Cummings was killed three years later, ironically, in an automobile accident on a quiet Indianapolis street.

For the second straight year, Chevrolet in Detroit sent advertising manager C. P. Fisken to award the prizes at the banquet. He personally welcomed each champ to Akron.

Every major radio network broadcast the race.

ROUND 1

The Preliminary Heats

Here, I recap some of the more meaningful heats of the first round. They are significant for an event that took place within the heat, the time posted, or an interesting fact about one or more of the contestants. The first round consisted of thirty-eight three-car heats and one heat of two cars.

Heat 1

Lane 1 John Sullivan, Bangor, ME
Lane 2 Elgan Dowell, Lafayette, IN
Lane 3 Merle Butts, Martinsburg, WV

In the first All-American heat ever run on the new Derby Downs track, Bangor's John Sullivan won with a time of 29.1 seconds. Hot on his heels was Elgan Dowell of Lafayette. Dowell had won in Lafayette by edging out the 1935 champ, Bill Heath, in the final heat.

Dowell–Lafayette Butts–Martinsburg Sullivan–Bangor

Heat 3

Lane 1 Leland Lewis, Binghamton, NY
Lane 2 Loren Cantrall, Springfield, IL
Lane 3 Robert McAndrew, Scranton, PA

The first of ten two-time champs—champs who had raced in the 1934 or 1935 All-American race—was Loren Cantrall. In 1935, he had won his first-round heat.

Heat 4

Lane 1 Donald Troutman, South Bend, IN
Lane 2 Richard Launder, Los Angeles, CA
Lane 3 Richard Snyder, Bloomington, IL

South Bend had done well in the 1935 All-American, so hopes were high that this young Hoosier would do likewise. He won his first heat by four car lengths. His winning time was twenty-nine seconds flat.

Heat 6

Lane 1 Raymond Merz, Oakland, CA
Lane 2 Arthur Boldt, Erie, PA
Lane 3 Paul Birbarie, New Haven, CT

Erie wins easily

This car won the best upholstery trophy

Heat 7

Lane 1 Eldon Morehouse, Memphis, TN
Lane 2 Alexander Fogg, Paterson, NJ
Lane 3 Wallace Dodge, Morgantown, WV

For fourteen-year-old Alex Fogg, who had also represented Paterson in 1935, the combination of a thirteen-hour train ride from New Jersey and the meals eaten on board proved too much for his stomach to handle. He spent his first night in Akron lying in his room on the thirteenth floor of the Mayflower Hotel. By Saturday, the two-time champ was ready to take part in the derby festivities. On Sunday, he piloted his orange racer to victory in heat 7, his main challenge coming from Eldon Morehouse of Memphis.

Memphis   Paterson   Morgantown

Heat 9

Lane 1 Winston Taylor, Spokane, WA
Lane 2 Junior Kendall, Portland, OR
Lane 3 Grant Heisler, Tulsa, OK

Portland's fifteen-year-old Junior Kendall showed he was a champ to watch, easily beating Taylor in a time of 28.4 seconds. Third in the heat was Grant Heisler, who was also the Tulsa Champ in 1935.

Junior Kendall

Heat 11

Lane 1 Bernard Kline, Ellwood City, PA
Lane 2 Earl Bishop, Manitowoc, WI
Lane 3 Ralph Everly, Dubuque, IA

Bernard Kline captured this unremarkable heat with ease. The only thing noteworthy was that the Dubuque car was modeled after "Old No. 7," the car pictured in the derby logo.

Ellwood City pulls away

Heat 12

Lane 1 William Mackey, Newark, NJ
Lane 2 Robert Turner, Muncie, IN
Lane 3 Raymond Stull, Fostoria, OH

The 1934 World Champion, Robert Turner, kept his hopes of a second title alive with a first-round win. He bested tiny "Skippy" Mackey in a slow time of 29.4 seconds.

Newark   Muncie   Fostoria

Heat 13

Lane 1 Robert Richards, Lima, OH
Lane 2 Franklin Schott, Milwaukee, WI
Lane 3 John Mayfield, Ann Arbor, MI

The first accident of the day took place in the unlucky thirteenth heat when the low-slung green racer belonging to Franklin Schott of Milwaukee swerved into the car driven by John Mayfield of Ann Arbor, went into a spin, and mashed heavily into the west guardrail. Schott suffered a slightly pulled back muscle. Mayfield escaped unhurt and was allowed to race again after his car had been repaired.

Robert Richards of Lima was unaffected by the mishap and won the heat with a great time of 28.4 seconds. His blue car bore on its side the insignia of the American Legion.

Heat 14

Lane 1 Charles Ballard, Akron, OH
Lane 2 Hansel Gray, Fort Smith, AR
Lane 3 Dale Studer, Dover, OH

Driving rainstorms had twice interrupted the running of Akron's local derby on Saturday, August 15, the day before the All-American. Finally, fifteen-year-old Charles Ballard, the son of an Akron attorney, was crowned champ in a field of 240 boys. His two-toned blue racer recorded consistently fast times throughout the day's racing. His brother, John, later served as mayor of Akron for fourteen years, from 1966 to 1979.

The partisan crowd's hopes were dashed early as Hansel Gray edged out to a three-foot lead over Ballard, with Studer another four feet back. Gray's lead gradually increased throughout the heat until his final margin was a car length over Ballard, with Studer another three lengths behind. With the local favorite eliminated, most of the Akron fans switched their allegiance to Robert Richards of Lima. He gave them a lot about which to cheer.

Akron   Fort Smith

Heat 15

Lane 1 Charles Bachman, Lansing, MI
Lane 2 Jack Dempsey, Little Rock, AR
Lane 3 Bill Bartlemess, Peekskill, NY

Heat 15 was an easy win for Lansing's Charles Bachman Jr. Charles was the son of legendary Michigan State football coach Charlie Bachman who was inducted into the College Football Hall of Fame in 1978. Young Charles posted one of the better times of the round, a 28.8 seconds.

Heat 15 inset—Coach Bachman

Heat 16

Lane 1 Roy Bible, Roanoke, VA
Lane 2 Kenneth Benton, Davenport, IA
Lane 3 Daniel Cannon, Rochester, NY

Nine-year-old Roy H. Bible had prevailed over a field of sixty-one contestants in Roanoke. A crowd of more than three-thousand watched as Bible piloted his silver, canvas-covered mount to victory. His slender car had posted the fastest times of each round to secure the win on the one-thousand-foot course in Roanoke. In the first round today, he coasted to a two-and-a-half-length win over Kenneth Benton of Davenport, with Rochester's Daniel Cannon another length back.

Roanoke   Davenport   Rochester

Heat 20

Lane 1 Wayne Collins, Indianapolis, IN
Lane 2 Eugene Mills, Helena, MT
Lane 3 Kenneth Walker, Altoona, PA

A portent of things to come, Wayne Collins was the first of three champs out of the Collins family to represent Indianapolis in the All–American.

Indianapolis   Helena   Altoona

Heat 21

Lane 1 Milton Levine, New York, NY
Lane 2 Earl Mosiman, Minneapolis, MN
Lane 3 Robert Marchand, Ft. Wayne, IN

Earl Mosiman reigned as the champion representing Minneapolis, just as he had the year before. This year he drove a totally different car. No longer fashioning his racer out of bicycles and a water tank, his creation was more conventional. But the result was the same, a first-round loss.

New York   Minneapolis   Ft. Wayne

Heat 23

Lane 1 Herbert Muench, St. Louis, MO
Lane 2 Robert Rowley, Waterbury, CT
Lane 3 Edmund Richardson, Detroit, MI

Edmund Richardson, who hailed from Royal Oak, Michigan, had entered and won the Detroit race in a car that was truly innovative. The nose was formed from half of an automobile headlight. The steering wheel rim featured a split garden hose to aid gripping. The wheels had saucepan hubcaps, and the body was constructed from a beer sign. It had a knee-action suspension system (see photo), which was popular in Detroit at that time. This racer was, without a doubt, the second-fastest car in the All-American race. Unfortunately, it was pitted against the eventual winner in the first round and lost by a narrow margin in the fastest heat of the day (28.2 seconds). This was a prime example of the *luck of the draw*. Herbert Muench, the son of a St. Louis X-ray specialist, had been victorious in St. Louis, edging out Gordon Miller of Granite City, Illinois, in the championship heat there. Miller was the brother of Everett Miller, who had represented St. Louis in the 1935 All-American and placed second, nationally, to Maurice Bale. Muench told reporters that it took him twenty-four days to build his black and red speedster in his basement. Once Muench had defeated Richardson, he had smooth sailing the rest of the day, never challenged in any heat. The third boy in the heat, Robert Rowley of Waterbury, was not a factor as he was beaten by thirty feet.

The fastest heat of the day

Richardson's Detroit car

Heat 24

Lane 1 Donald Zbinden, Wadsworth, OH
Lane 2 Bobby Harris, Youngstown, OH
Lane 3 Harold Holsapple, Vincennes, IN

Donald Zbinden traveled a mere sixteen miles from neighboring Wadsworth to Akron to compete. His racing day came to an abrupt halt when a worn grommet in the steering assembly of his red racer caused him to lose control and crash into the guardrail on the east side of the track.

Bobby Harris, who was also the 1935 Youngstown champ, avoided colliding with Zbinden and finished the heat. But the winner was fourteen-year-old Harold Holsapple, who had triumphed in a field of thirty-four in Vincennes by defeating his thirteen-year-old brother, Charles, in the final heat.

Heat 24 just before Zbinden (left) crashed

Heat 27

Lane 1 George Collella, Boston, MA
Lane 2 P. Ramon Yeager, Cleveland, OH
Lane 3 Val Decot, Buffalo, NY

The most severe crash of the day took place when twelve-year-old Ramon Yeager, who fought to gain control of his racer throughout his heat, smashed into the kickboard four hundred feet from the finish line. The impact hurled Yeager into the arms of spectators in the stands. He received a few bruises on his back and legs, but the most damage was to his pride. He had made the trip to Akron from Cleveland on the Goodyear blimp. The heat was captured by Val Decot (pronounced *dee*-co) of Buffalo, whose younger brother, Buddy, had been the 1935 Buffalo champ. Their father was a surgeon famous for being the first doctor to remove a human eyeball, work on it, replace it in the socket, and have it work perfectly.

Boston   Cleveland   Buffalo

Yeager unties his racer from the Goodyear blimp

Heat 29

Lane 1 Maurice Bale, Anderson, IN
Lane 2 Frederick Huss, Terre Haute, IN
Lane 3 Robert Schwartz, Passaic, NJ

The quest for a second national championship by Maurice Bale remained intact after the first round, as he won by a full five lengths in the time of twenty-nine seconds flat. Bale had constructed an entirely new racer since the car in which he won the 1935 All-American became the property of Chevrolet.

A composite of heat 29

Heat 30

Lane 1 Buddy Bankey, Toledo, OH
Lane 2 Harold Hansen, White Plains, NY
Lane 3 George Partlow, Philadelphia, PA

Two repeat champs competed in heat 30. Buddy Bankey had built a new racer for 1936 that was a copy of Maurice Bale's winning car from 1935. He was pitted against Harold Hansen, who had barely been edged out by Akron's Loney Kline on Tallmadge Hill the previous year.

This was one of the tightest races of the first round as Hansen edged Bankey by less than half a car length. His time was a solid 28.6 seconds.

White Plains edges out Toledo

Bankey's racer

Heat 31

Lane 1 Paul Brown, Oklahoma City, OK
Lane 2 Frank Caiazzo, Union City, NJ
Lane 3 Russell Scott, San Francisco, CA

Once again, two repeat champs vied in the same heat. One was Paul Brown, who had created quite a stir nationally the year before by running into famous announcers Graham McNamee and Tom Manning while they were announcing the race over national radio. The other was Frank Caiazzo, who had constructed his racer by following plans that were published in *Popular Mechanics* magazine. Caiazzo's winning time was 29.2 seconds.

Oklahoma City   Union City   San Francisco

Russell Scott

Heat 32

Lane 1 John Korb, San Diego, CA
Lane 2 Thomas Darnall, Buckhannon, WV
Lane 3 Robert Purcell, Wichita, KS

The only notable fact about heat 32 was that the champ racing in lane three was named Robert Purcell, and he hailed from Wichita. That doesn't seem particularly remarkable except that heat 5 also had a lad named Robert Purcell, and he represented Bloomington, Indiana. Both Purcells were beaten in the first round, eliminating any chance of confusion in the finals.

San Diego   Buckhannon   Wichita

Heat 33

Lane 1 Richard Brown, Grafton, WV
Lane 2 Herman Brown, Macon, GA
Lane 3 Walter Williams, Nashville, TN

Early in the first round, it became apparent that any winning time under twenty-nine seconds was very good. So when Walter Williams posted a 28.8 in winning this heat, the spectators made a mental note. The lanky fourteen-year-old modeled his blue car after Captain Malcolm Campbell's famous Bluebird racer in which he had set land-speed records. The blue Nashville race car still exists and was recently sold on eBay.

Grafton   Macon   Nashville

Heat 34

Lane 1 Wilbur Cramblet, Wheeling, WV
Lane 2 John Tabor, Pittsburgh, PA
Lane 3 Gene Townsend, Topeka, KS

Fifteen-year-old Wilbur Cramblet found, upon winning the Wheeling city race, that one of the prizes was a trip to Pittsburgh to watch the city race there. Wilbur was the son of Dr. W. H. Cramblet, president of Bethany College. In Pittsburgh he watched John Tabor consistently record the fastest times in winning. Tabor piloted a racer that resembled the *Hindenburg* airship. On All-American race day, Cramblet found that his first-round opponent would be none other than John Tabor. The Pittsburgh champ took the heat with the fast time of 28.8 seconds.

Pittsburgh's John Tabor

Heat 37

Lane 1 Thomas Howard, Atlanta, GA
Lane 2 Albert Guenther, Benton Harbor, MI
Lane 3 Dick Yentzer, Sheridan, WY

Atlanta's champ, thirteen-year-old Tom Howard, caught the eyes of spectators near the starting line with his unique driving style. As the starting blocks fell, Tom let go of the steering wheel and pumped his fists in the air to try to gain momentum. In addition, he drove barefoot. He won his heat easily, but his time was not among the day's best.

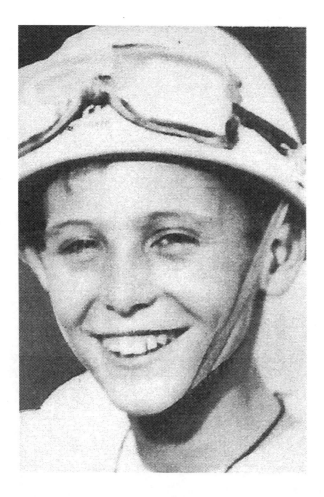

Tom Howard

Heat 39

Lane 1 John Dobson, Deadwood, SD
Lane 2 Robert Mahan, Jamaica, NY

Mahan, who actually lived in Flushing Meadows, entered the Long Island race and topped a field of 218 contestants. The fourteen-hour ride to Akron proved too much for him to handle. He spent a very ill first day at the Mayflower Hotel, and his roomies there were the 1934 and1935 world champs, Robert Turner and Maurice Bale. This, Mahan hoped, was a sign of good things to come. He scored a four-length victory over John Dobson. His time of 30.4 seconds did not place him among the favorites.

Heat 40

Lane 2 Bert Varian, Boise, ID
Lane 3 John Mayfield, Ann Arbor, MI

This was a special heat created for Varian, who was scratched from heat 5, and Mayfield, who was fouled in heat 13. In winning the heat, Varian recorded the slowest winning time of the day at 30.8 seconds.

Varian edges out Mayfield

With the first round concluded, all of the racers had been seen. Spectators were picking their favorites based on first-round times. The fastest times of the round were as follows:

- 28.2 seconds by Muench of St. Louis
- 28.4 seconds by Wishart of Knoxville
- 28.4 seconds by Kendall of Portland
- 28.4 seconds by Richards of Lima
- 28.6 seconds by Collins of Indianapolis
- 28.6 seconds by Marchand of Ft. Wayne

- 28.6 seconds by Hansen of White Plains
- 28.6 seconds by Harrold of Peoria

The fastest eight cars were within 0.4 seconds of each other. Five others had registered 28.8 seconds and could not be ruled out. It would take another round before things would really come into focus.

ROUND 2

//

This round consisted of fourteen heats matching first-round winners who drew for the lanes in which they would race.

Heat 41

Lane 1 Loren Cantrall, Springfield, IL
Lane 2 Paul Wishart, Knoxville, TN
Lane 3 John Sullivan, Bangor, ME

Springfield's Cantrall was leading by half a car length when Wishart lost control of his racer and swerved into Cantrall, knocking him out of line. Cantrall managed to get clear for a second, but Wishart's car swerved again, striking Cantrall's back wheel, sending him into the guardrail, cracking a wheel, and bending his axle, making it impossible for him to continue. That enabled Sullivan to cross the finish line alone. His winning time was 29.1 seconds. But for the collision, Cantrall would probably have recorded a better winning time.

Herman Brown of Macon, Georgia, who had been beaten in heat 33, offered his red-and-black racer to Cantrall so he could continue. After one of the heats, while the cars were being towed up the hill, the track announcer told the crowd of Herman's splendid offer. Thousands of people cheered as the towheaded youngster grinned bashfully, and his parents beamed proudly. So although Herman was not acclaimed as a racing champion, he was recognized as a champion sportsman. The technical committee was forced to refuse the offer under the race regulation that each boy must drive a car he built.

Heat 42

Lane 1 Arthur Boldt, Erie, PA
Lane 2 Donald Troutman, South Bend, IN
Lane 3 Earl Hudson, Portland, ME

Troutman didn't equal his first-round time, but he did edge out Boldt for the win.

Erie   South Bend   Portland

Heat 43

Lane 1 Junior Kendall, Portland, OR
Lane 2 Leonard Dyer, Lexington, KY
Lane 3 Alex Fogg, Paterson, NJ

It was a five-car-length win for Junior Kendall in a time of 28.8 seconds.

Kendall wins going away

Heat 44

Lane 1 Robert Turner, Muncie, IN
Lane 2 Bernard Kline, Ellwood City, PA
Lane 3 Berkley Harper, Kansas City, KS

Robert Turner's hopes of being a two-time world champ came apart, as did his right rear wheel halfway through heat 44. He was running neck and neck with Berkley Harper when the mishap occurred. Only skillful driving averted a crash. Harper went on to win, posting a time of thirty seconds flat.

Heat 45

Lane 1 Robert Richards, Lima, OH
Lane 2 Hansel Gray, Fort Smith, AR
Lane 3 Charles Bachman, Lansing, MI

Richards got the attention of the crowd as he set the fastest mark of the second round, 28.4 seconds.

Heat 46

Lane 1 Roy Bible, Roanoke, VA
Lane 2 Courtney Cook, Denver, CO
Lane 3 Robert King, Columbia, SC

The outcome of this heat was predictable—Bible's first-round win was a full second faster than King's and 0.6 seconds faster than Cook's. In addition, he bettered his own time in this heat.

Heat 47

Lane 1 Wayne Collins, Indianapolis, IN
Lane 2 Robert Marchand, Ft. Wayne, IN
Lane 3 Joe Cheskevich, Chicago, IL

Collins and Marchand had recorded identical times in the first round, so it follows that this would be a tight one—and it was. Marchand was a game competitor, but the road-hugging racer of Collins edged out to a half-length win. His time once again was 28.6 seconds.

Heat 48

Lane 1 Herbert Muench, St. Louis, MO
Lane 2 Harold Holsapple, Vincennes, IN
Lane 3 Warren Lantz, Harrisburg, PA

Herbert Muench didn't match his first-round time, but his 28.8 seconds was more than fast enough to win by his biggest margin of the day.

Heat 49

Lane 1 Richard Moore, Bridgeport, CT
Lane 2 Don Getchell, Rapid City, SD
Lane 3 Val Decot, Buffalo, NY

Although Richard Moore didn't equal his first-round time, neither did his opponents. He won easily.

Heat 50

Lane 1 Harold Hansen, White Plains, NY
Lane 2 Ellsworth Staley, Tacoma, WA
Lane 3 Maurice Bale, Anderson, IN

Just like Robert Turner, Maurice Bale saw his dream of a second world championship slip away. Harold Hansen opened up a two-car lead and was increasing it when he reached the finish line. His time of 28.8 seconds was quite respectable. As in the first round, Hansen defeated a repeat champ from 1935.

Heat 51

Lane 1 John Korb, San Diego, CA
Lane 2 Walter Williams, Nashville, TN
Lane 3 Frank Caiazzo, Union City, NJ

Twenty-nine seconds flat was the mark achieved by Walter Williams, but it got him the win in heat 51—and by a comfortable margin.

Heat 52

Lane 1 John Tabor, Pittsburgh, PA
Lane 2 Norman Harrold, Peoria, IL
Lane 3 Glidden Doman, Syracuse, NY

John Tabor drew lane one and by the four-hundred-foot mark he already had a big lead. It grew larger until, at the finish stripe, he was ahead by five lengths.

Heat 53

Lane 2 Thomas Howard, Atlanta, GA
Lane 3 Dean Marty, New Martinsville, WV

Howard eclipsed his first-round mark as he scored an impressive win over Marty.
His elapsed time in this two-car affair was 28.8 seconds.

Heat 54

Lane 2 Bert Varian, Boise, ID
Lane 3 Robert Mahan, Jamaica, NY

The last heat of the second round was also a two-racer contest. In taking the heat, Mahan tied Varian for the slowest winning time, a snail-like 30.8 seconds.

That concluded the second round, in which only five of the fourteen winners broke the twenty-nine-second barrier.

ROUND 3

///

This round was only five heats. Once the five winners were determined, they would then jockey to see who would place first through fifth.

Heat 55

Lane 1 Junior Kendall, Portland, OR
Lane 2 John Sullivan, Bangor, ME
Lane 3 Donald Troutman, South Bend, IN

Although Junior Kendall posted his slowest time, he still took the flag by nipping Troutman at the stripe.

Heat 56

Lane 1 Roy Bible, Roanoke, VA
Lane 2 Berkley Harper, Kansas City, KS
Lane 3 Robert Richards, Lima, OH

The order of finish was Richards, Bible, and Harper. Lima's champ matched his second-round time of 28.4 in defeating the slender racer from Roanoke.

Heat 57

Lane 1 Herbert Muench, St. Louis, MO
Lane 2 Wayne Collins, Indianapolis, IN
Lane 3 Richard Moore, Bridgeport, CT

Two tenths of a second was the difference as Muench prevailed over Collins. The St. Louis champ's time was 28.4 seconds. Collins, for the third straight time, posted a 28.6. Moore, who had not cracked 29 seconds in either of his heats, trailed Collins by another two car lengths.

Heat 58

Lane 1 Walter Williams, Nashville, TN
Lane 2 Harold Hansen, White Plains, IN
Lane 3 John Tabor, Pittsburgh, PA

The order of finish was Hansen, Williams, and Tabor. Hansen's black racer posted a winning time of 28.6 seconds.

Nashville and White Plains ready to roll

Heat 59

Lane 2 Robert Mahan, Jamaica, NY
Lane 3 Thomas Howard, Atlanta, GA

Although Thomas Howard made the top five with this win, his times were not impressive, and the thirty seconds flat he set in heat 59 did nothing to enhance his chances in the finals.

ROUND 4

Now the five finalists had been determined. Those at trackside were comparing winning times.

Heat 60

Lane 1 Robert Richards, Lima, OH
Lane 2 Herbert Muench, St. Louis, MO
Lane 3 Junior Kendall, Portland, OR

As the three racers progressed down the incline, the Lima car, in lane one, drifted a bit toward lane two, as did the Portland car in lane three. At the halfway point, Muench opened up a two-foot lead over Richards, with Kendall lagging another five feet back. Muench held steady in the center of lane two. As they crossed the stripe, it was St. Louis over Lima by four feet, with Portland two lengths back.

Muench would be in the championship heat! His time: 28.4 seconds.

St. Louis edges Lima; Portland trails

Heat 61

Lane 2 Harold Hansen, White Plains, NY
Lane 3 Thomas Howard, Atlanta, GA

Observers felt this heat would not be close, based on previous times, and they were right. Hansen secured his place in the championship heat with an easy win over Howard in an elapsed time of 28.6 seconds.

The start of the other fourth-round heat; note Howard's driving style

Author's Note

A few procedures were handled poorly in the 1936 race. First, the eliminations were set up in such a way that the top five places were awarded instead of the top six. A better plan would have been to stage a three-car heat to determine fourth, fifth, and sixth and then a three-car championship heat. This is the way it is done nowadays. The progression builds to a natural climax. However, in 1936, there was a certain amount of trial and error, and the championship heat, a two-car affair, was run before the heat to determine third, fourth, and fifth, making the semifinal heat anticlimactic. Second, the heats listed in the program did not have the racers in the correct lanes, nor did it list the car numbers. This caused some confusion. And finally, the champs were not allowed to take a trial run before race day. This may have been a factor in the three collisions during the race.

ROUND 5

The American Championship

The Championship Heat

Heat 62

Lane 1 Harold Hansen, White Plains, NY
Lane 3 Herbert Muench, St. Louis, MO

Harold Hansen had spent $9.76 to construct his black racer, while Muench had shelled out $9.92 to build his red and black speedster. As the starting blocks fell, the two young hopefuls hunched over in their cars trying to eliminate wind resistance. It was anyone's race for the first three hundred feet. Then the St. Louis car crept out to a slight edge. At the halfway point, the White Plains car wavered a little, its wheels edging into lane two. From that point on, Muench continued to increase his lead until the two swept across the finish line. Two car lengths was the final margin for the Missourian as the crowd thundered its approval. His time again was 28.4 seconds. As he was brought back to the finish line to be interviewed, an attractive figure in green darted through the crowd. She could hardly wait to get to the side of her son. There in front of three hundred newsmen, she smothered the grimy-faced young Herbert with kisses. A state highway patrol motorcycle officer brought the father, a physician, down the track in a side car. He grabbed the boy and kissed him too.

St. Louis takes the championship

Third, Fourth, Fifth

Heat 63

Lane 1 Junior Kendall, Portland, OR
Lane 2 Thomas Howard, Atlanta, GA
Lane 3 Robert Richards, Lima, OH

Much of the partisan crowd had switched its allegiance to the Lima champ after Akron's Charles Ballard was eliminated. Since Richards was the only Ohio boy left in the race, they roared their approval as he swept to a two-and-a-half-car-length victory to take third place. Junior Kendall of Portland captured fourth with a three-length margin over Atlanta's Tom Howard.

Portland   Atlanta   Lima

Lima over Portland with Atlanta trailing

All that remained was the international heat for the championship of the world. But before it was run, Norman Neumann was given a trial run. The thinking here was that Muench and Hansen had the advantage of having already driven on the track and that a practice run would negate that advantage. But it became obvious that Neumann's car could not meet the competition provided by Muench and Hansen. He was clocked at 29.2 seconds.

THE INTERNATIONAL CHAMPIONSHIP

Heat 64

Lane 1 Herbert Muench, St. Louis, MO
Lane 2 Harold Hansen, White Plains, NY
Lane 3 Norman Neumann, Pretoria, South Africa

The White Plains contingent hoped that Muench's victory in the US championship heat was due to the lanes not being equal. This was not the case. This time the St. Louis champ, racing in lane one, coasted to another decisive victory over Hansen, with Neumann a distant third. The time was 28.6 seconds.

St. Louis takes it all

THE BANQUET

That evening the banquet was held at the Mayflower Hotel in downtown Akron, the same building that housed the champs during race week. After dinner, the first order of business was the announcement that the derby would again be held in Akron in 1937. This was a practice for many years but nowadays it is assumed. Then C. P. Fisken, who earlier in the week had personally welcomed each champ to Akron, presented each participant with a racing certificate from Chevrolet.

This certificate went to Muench

Next, the celebrities made short speeches congratulating the boys on their sportsmanship and on doing a fine job of racing. The next order of business was the special awards. The car that was deemed to be the best balanced was the one built by Ellery Carlson of Sioux City.

Carlson gets his award

The construction and design trophy went to Pittsburgh's John Tabor

Tabor receives his trophy

The fastest-heat trophy went to Muench for his posting of 28.2 seconds in the first round

The best upholstered car was that of Arthur Boldt of Erie

Arthur Boldt

Paul Brown had the best brakes

Paul Brown

Next was the awarding of the placers. Fifth place was captured by Tom Howard of Atlanta.

Tom Howard

Fourth place went to Junior Kendall of Portland.
The top three were brought up together and awarded their trophies.

Muench Hansen Richards

The Winners, 1936

While the Derby program awarded only the top five places, I have taken the liberty of awarding sixth through tenth place based on recorded heat times, the method used in later years. The top ten goes as follows.

First	Herbert Muench	St. Louis
Second	Harold Hansen	White Plains
Third	Robert Richards	Lima
Fourth	Junior Kendall	Portland
Fifth	Thomas Howard	Atlanta
Sixth	Wayne Collins	Indianapolis
Seventh	Walter Williams	Nashville
Eighth	Donald Troutman	South Bend
Ninth	Roy Bible	Roanoke
Tenth	Robert Mahan	Jamaica Long Island

The prize list was lengthy.

First	$2,000 scholarship to any state college or university
	National championship trophy
	Gold Derby medal—Diamond set
Second	Chevrolet Master Coach
	National second-place trophy
	Silver Derby medal—Ruby set
Third	Chevrolet Standard Coach
	National third-place trophy
	Bronze Derby medal—Sapphire set
Fourth	Victor 16mm motion picture camera and projector
	National fourth-place silver trophy
Fifth	Set of Edwin T. Hamilton handicraft books

International trophies
First-place trophy to the winner of the international heat
Second-place trophy
Third-place trophy

Upon the conclusion of the banquet, many of the champs and their families began the journey home. Most of the ones who lived far from Akron opted to stay and get a good night's rest before beginning the long treks back to their own states. The one thing that they all had in common, win or lose, was five days of great memories. Chevrolet, the *Akron Beacon Journal,* and all the hundreds of volunteers who made it happen had done a remarkable job.

FOLLOW-UP

Herbert Muench: Winner

1936 World Champ

Accounts differ as to Muench's top speed. Estimates run as high as fifty-five miles per hour and as low as thirty-six. I believe forty-two miles per hour to be an accurate number. Muench didn't use his scholarship immediately after high school. He was drafted and served in the US Army in Europe during World War II. After returning home, he settled in Washington state, where he attended night school and earned a bachelor's of science in mechanical engineering. He became a widower and later remarried, and then he spent the last few years of his life in Salem, Oregon, where he passed away at the age of seventy-nine.

Muench later in life

His recollection of the local race in St. Louis was a bit hazy. He remembered winning that race by a large margin when, in fact, he barely nipped Gordon Miller for the championship.

Start of the final heat in St. Louis

The finish of the heat

But he was right on the money about his first-round opponent in Akron. He stated that Edmund Richardson of Detroit was his toughest competition and should have placed second, but since he was beaten in the first round, he was out. Muench returned to Akron several times as a guest of the Derby and stated that the former champs were always treated royally.

Harold Hansen: Runner-Up

1936 Runner-up

Harold, who had represented White Plains in the 1935 All-American race, improved vastly on his performance in 1936. The lanky fifteen-year-old wanted to attend the US Naval Academy in Annapolis and pursue a military career with the scholarship money he planned to receive from the Derby. Now he would have to find another means of funding that dream. He did, however, win a new Chevrolet. "I can drive a car," he stated, "but my dad doesn't like me to." His mother and father couldn't make the trip to Akron but were tuned in to the race on the radio. Young Hansen was the first to congratulate Muench on his victory. He was president of his class in school.

Robert Richards: Third Place

A stray dog spelled trouble for fourteen-year-old Robert Richards. The mutt picked an inopportune time to run onto the track—the championship heat in Lima's local race. After crossing the finish line, Richards tried unsuccessfully to avoid the pooch and lost control flipping his racer over. He incurred some nasty facial cuts, and when he was photographed being presented his trophy, his face was heavily bandaged.

Richards after the mishap

The Crowd

Estimates of the size of the crowd ranged from 75,000 to more than 100,000. The latter figure was that of the Akron police and was based on the fact that 24,000 cars were parked at or near Derby Downs. I believe 50,000 to be a more accurate estimate since attendance reports were always inflated.

PART 2

PROLOGUE

The World in 1937

Internationally, Neville Chamberlain became prime minister of England, and Japan invaded China.

Here at home, unemployment dropped for the second year in a row and was now at 14.3 percent. In January, Franklin Roosevelt was inaugurated for his second term, and *Look* Magazine was introduced to the public. In the world of aviation, Howard Hughes set a new record for transcontinental flight by traveling from Los Angeles to New York in seven hours, twenty-eight minutes, and twenty-five seconds. America received the tragic news that Amelia Earhart vanished while trying to become the first woman to fly around the world, and we witnessed the Hindenburg disaster at Lakehurst, New Jersey.

On the radio, the first installment of *The Shadow* aired. On the silver screen, Daffy Duck debuted, as did *Snow White and the Seven Dwarfs*, the first feature-length animated film. And the Oscar for best picture was awarded to *The Life of Emile Zola*.

In the literary world, Steinbeck's *Of Mice and Men* hit the bookstores, as did *The Hobbit* by J. R. R. Tolkien and Agatha Christie's *Death on the Nile*.

In the world of sports, War Admiral won the Kentucky Derby, and Joe Louis knocked out Jim Braddock to become the heavyweight champion. The Yankees took the World Series over the Giants four games to one. And finally, Pittsburgh claimed the NCAA football championship.

The cost of living rose somewhat, as the average home cost $4,100 and a comparable car ran $760. People budgeted money to afford rents of twenty-six dollars a month, hamburger meat at twelve cents a pound, gasoline at ten cents a gallon, and bread at nine cents a loaf on an average yearly American income of $1,780. A new product called Spam was produced by Hormel.

Notables born that year include Jack Nicholson, Morgan Freeman, Anthony Hopkins, Bill Cosby, Dustin Hoffman, Vanessa Redgrave, Jane Fonda, Dyan Cannon, and Roger Penske.

Those who passed away include George Gershwin, Jean Harlow, Guglielmo Marconi, and Colin Clive.

DERBY DOWNS COMES OF AGE

In January of 1937, Myron Scott returned to the *Dayton Daily News,* and J. P. Gormley assumed directorship of the race. The rules committee revised the age limits to range from nine to fifteen years old. But the biggest change was that former city champions were barred from racing again.

Car building had changed radically by 1937. The emphasis was now on such factors as balance, weight distribution, lubricants, bearings, streamlining, steering design, and brake construction. The B. F. Goodrich Company, which had done much work in perfecting sets of wheels and axles, sold these sets on a nonprofit basis at $6.00 to $6.95 a set. At Derby Downs, a new steel, double-decked bridge with a floor space of nine hundred square feet replaced the wooden one. The seating facilities were improved, and new photo finish and timing equipment was installed. With the new setup, the timing apparatus was tripped when the starting blocks fell and stopped when the nose of the first racer interrupted a light beam across the finish line. This also triggered the photo-finish camera looking down upon the finish stripe from high on the bridge. Through the first three years of the All-American, there had never been a heat so close that a photo was needed to determine the winner. In 1937, that would change.

A total of 620 Chevrolet dealers participated in the program, and the 120 local races drew an estimated 1.5 million spectators and 25,000 entrants. Canada and Hawaii joined the competition for the first time. Unlike the previous year, the champs were given the opportunity to try out the track before actually competing. These test runs were held on Saturday.

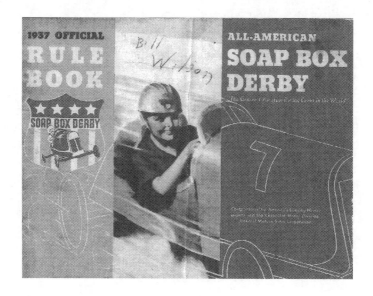

The 1937 rule book

Celebrities

On hand again were Rickenbacker, Hartz, McNamee, and Manning. Ted Husing described the race on nationwide radio. After concluding his broadcast, he stated,

> This is the tops. I've seen sports events of every nature. I've never seen anything like this in all my life. I have studied hard for many years to become able to describe pictures, but this show almost baffles me. The thrilling climax to which it works; the smoothness with which it operates; the split-second precision in the running of the heats; the pageantry of the bands and color units; the thrill of looking down from the bridge upon a sea of persons—I'm telling you there isn't anything like it.

Famed Indy 500 winner Wilbur Shaw made the first of many appearances at Derby Downs. The following is an excerpt from his autobiography, *Gentlemen, Start Your Engines.*

> Harry Hartz was responsible for my first appearance at the Soap Box Derby Finals. He had been invited to serve as official starter for the 1937 event, a few weeks after I had scored my first "500" victory and he asked me to accompany him. I was fairly certain I could have a lot more fun doing something else that weekend, but Harry was insistent. "You'll really enjoy it, Wilbur," he said. "The kids are wonderful to work with, and the race means as much to them as the '500' does to us." I finally agreed to go and got one of the biggest thrills of my life out of that first trip to the Derby Finals. I've been a regular ever since, officiating at all but two of the events, when it was impossible for me to attend. In my opinion, it's the finest competition in the world for boys. Chevrolet certainly deserves all of the publicity it receives for sponsoring the nation-wide program. I'll be the proudest dad in all of the United States if Bill can win it when he becomes old enough to take part. In addition to stimulating the development of skill and sportsmanship, it emphasizes the value of ingenuity and perseverance.

Race Week

Articles appeared daily in the *Akron Beacon Journal* previewing the upcoming race. The artwork was good, and the pictures were plentiful. By Sunday everything had been set.

Some of the artwork

Prerace hype

The cars

More cars

Race Day

Race day, August 15, 1937, was warm and sunny as 120 boys anxiously awaited their chance at fame. With the giant prerace parade and the national anthem concluded, it was time for racing.

I have recapped only the heats that help tell the story. I have omitted those that had no bearing on how the winner was determined.

ROUND 1

The Preliminary Heats

Heat 2

Lane 1 Charles Kerst, Cleveland, OH
Lane 2 Hugh Flury, Atlanta, GA
Lane 3 Walter Ritchey, Pittsburgh, PA

Ritchey lost control of his vehicle shortly after the start and smashed into the west guardrail. He was unhurt, and Flury won the heat going away, in a winning time of 29.15 seconds. It became apparent early that any winning time under thirty seconds was very good.

Atlanta   Cleveland   Pittsburgh

Heat 8

Lane 1 John Harris, Charleston, WV
Lane 2 Kenneth Richardson, Detroit, MI
Lane 3 Horace Jackson, Harrisburg, PA

Kenneth Richardson (the brother of 1936 Detroit champ Edmund) was the victor in this heat by at least ten car lengths. The crowd made a mental note of his winning time of 29.45. This heat also marked the first appearance of Charleston in the All-American. Although John Harris didn't fare well today, Charleston would be a real force in derby racing in later years.

Richardson of Detroit far out in front

Author's note: Comparing winning times from one year to another is pointless. Wind, temperature, humidity, and many other factors combine to skew any conclusions. While average winning times were better in 1936, this does not mean that the cars were faster that year. In fact, the opposite was true.

Heat 12

Lane 1 Andy Rummel, Helena, MT
Lane 2 Stuart Crouch, Louisville, KY
Lane 3 Jack Kendall, Portland, OR

Thirteen-year-old Jack Kendall (brother of 1936 champ Junior Kendall) scored another lopsided win in heat 12—his time was 29.40 seconds.

The start of heat 12

Heat 14

Lane 1 Donald Armstrong, Newark, NJ
Lane 2 Robert Ballard, White Plains, NY
Lane 3 James Hamme, Bay City, MI

Robert Ballard of White Plains recorded the fastest time of the day in winning this heat. He accomplished this despite weaving within his lane. His time was 28.86 seconds.

Ballard alone at the finish line

Heat 20

Lane 1 Wayne Handley, North Platte, NE
Lane 2 Dwight Davis, Fort Wayne, IN
Lane 3 Chester Plegge, St. Louis, MO

Chester Plegge won in St. Louis with a car that was entirely enclosed. He drove with his legs completely flexed and steered by reaching around his knees.

He took heat 20 in a time of 29.15 seconds, the second best of the round. Chester, age fourteen, had survived two wrecks and a broken wheel in winning his local race. He came to Akron in the hope of defending the world championship won the previous year by Herbert Muench.

Plegge's enclosed racer; note his hands and knees

Heat 41

Lane 1 John Sigmans, Bethlehem, PA
Lane 3 Paul Jenkins, Scranton, PA

Twelve-year-old John Sigmans fell ill upon his arrival in town and was taken to Akron's Children's Hospital, where he was kept overnight. As a result, he missed taking his trial run on Saturday. Early Sunday morning, he was released and took his practice run before the day's festivities began. He captured the last heat of the first round with a good time of 29.85 seconds.

Now the field of 120 boys had been reduced to 41. Only the faster cars remained.

The heats would be closer. The average times would be better. Only nine times had the thirty-second barrier been broken. The second round would consist of fourteen heats. Few photos of the second round are available, but the notable victors and their winning times follow.

ROUND 2

The second round saw six of its fourteen winners post times under thirty seconds.

Heat 42 Hugh Flury, Atlanta, GA—29.22

Heat 44 Kenneth Richardson, Detroit, MI—29.49

Heat 45 Jack Kendall, Portland, OR—29.53

Heat 46 Robert Ballard, White Plains, IN—29.21

Heat 48 Chester Plegge, St. Louis, MO—29.45

Heat 51 Eugene Kinkade, New Martinsville, WV—28.92

The forty-fifth heat was interesting in that all three of its contestants had posted times under thirty seconds in the first round. In that heat, Jack Kendall bested Jack Bishop of Topeka and Warren Hodosko of Lima.

Jack Kendall, winner of heat 45

Heat 49–a typical photo-finish picture

Start of heat 54

Akron   South Bend   San Francisco

ROUND 3

This round consisted of six heats. All six winners would take home trophies for placing.

Heat 56

Atlanta's Flury beat Eugene Millard of Bloomington, Illinois, by a car length.

Heat 57

Detroit's Richardson edged out Jack Kendall of Portland.

Heat 58

Robert Ballard recorded his second time under 29 seconds with a 28.92 in beating Joe Wood of Columbus, Georgia.

Heat 59

Chester Plegge scored an easy victory over Billy Kindrick of Little Rock.

Heat 60

Oakland's Justin Hensley edged Eugene Kinkade of New Martinsville in a close heat. Third was John Sternbergh of Seattle, Washington.

Hensley scores a third-round win

Heat 61

Although Akron's Billy Wilson had won two heats, his times were poor.
This fact was borne out as he was easily topped by Sigmans of Bethlehem.

Sigmans wins heat 61

ROUND 4

Now six boys were left. All were assured of placing. The round would consist of three two-car heats to determine who would race in the championship heat.

Heat 62

Lane 1 Kenneth Richardson, Detroit, MI
Lane 3 Hugh Flury, Atlanta, GA

The two speeding cars hit the finish stripe simultaneously, so far as the human eye could see. This would be a job for the photo-finish camera, but when the picture was developed, a winner could still not be determined. It would have to be rerun. The rerun was nearly as close, but the Detroit car barely edged the Atlanta racer to qualify for the championship heat.

Harry Hartz flags the dead heat; this photo shows only one wheel of the Atlanta car

Heat 63

Lane 1 Robert Ballard, White Plains, IN
Lane 3 Chester Plegge, St. Louis, MO

Both boys drove poorly. Ballard, in lane one, wavered throughout the heat. As his blue speedster crossed the finish line, two of his wheels were in lane two. Plegge veered steadily to his right in lane three and finished the heat with his entire car in lane two. There was no danger of a collision, however, because Ballard had opened up a three-length lead.

Start of heat 63

Heat 64

Lane 1 Justin Hensley, Oakland, CA
Lane 3 John Sigmans, Bethlehem, PA

John Sigmans assured himself of a spot in the final heat with a two-car-length victory over Justin Hensley.

Heat 64 nears the finish line

Author's note: There was no heat to determine fourth, fifth, and sixth. These places were awarded based on winning times.

ROUND 5

The Championship Heat

Heat 65

Lane 1 John Sigmans, Bethlehem, PA
Lane 2 Kenneth Richardson, Detroit, MI
Lane 3 Robert Ballard, White Plains, IN

Robert Ballard had become a solid favorite, having bettered the twenty-nine-second mark three times. Only one other car had done it once, and that boy had been eliminated. Still, Ballard's poor driving was worrisome. The three 12-year-olds sat poised in their homemade autos while flashbulbs popped. The crowd stood and watched as the starting blocks fell. Once again, Ballard quickly took the lead, but as in his early heats, he was weaving. He did so throughout the heat, but it didn't matter. His superior racer was not to be denied. When he crossed the finish line, his car was partially in lane two, but he had a comfortable lead over Richardson.

Sigmans trailed Richardson by twenty feet to finish third. Ballard was brought back to the finish line and presented with the United States championship trophy, but his work was far from finished. There was still a little matter of the international race.

Sigmans, Richardson, and Ballard

The finish

Ballard and Richardson

International Semifinal

Heat 66

Lane 1 Danie Wege, South Africa
Lane 2 George Wilson, Toronto
Lane 3 John Frieteria, Hawaii

The first- and second-place winners in this heat would race against Ballard in the international heat. Wege was first, and Frieteria was second.

The international semifinal

The International Final

Heat 67

Lane 1 Danie Wege, South Africa
Lane 2 John Frieteria, Hawaii
Lane 3 Robert Ballard, White Plains, IN

Ballard did his poorest driving of the day in this heat. At the two-hundred-feet mark he swerved into lane two, only to make a left turn back into lane three. Still, it was of no consequence as he won the heat by about sixty feet. He was now truly the World Champion.

Wege, Frieteria, and Ballard

International finish

There was a wild scene when Ballard won. Photographers, reporters, and radio broadcasters plus scores of curious fans crowded onto the track and surrounded the champion as he posed for round after round of pictures. Ballard's father, Lewis, a real estate broker in White Plains, told reporters, "I'm afraid you're going to have another Ballard back here next year because my other boy, Richard, has a car that's really faster than Bobby's. Both boys spent 150 hours building their cars, but believe me, it was worth it."[1]

THE BANQUET

As in the previous year, the banquet was held in the ballroom of the Akron's Mayflower Hotel. Few photos still exist, but the same format was followed as in 1936.

The Winners, 1937

While the derby program awarded only the top six places, once again I have taken the liberty of awarding seventh through tenth place based on winning times of earlier heats. My final top ten goes as follows:

First	Robert Ballard	White Plains
Second	Kenneth Richardson	Detroit
Third	John Sigmans	Bethlehem
Fourth	Chester Plegge	St. Louis
Fifth	Hugh Flury	Atlanta
Sixth	Justin Hensley	Oakland
Seventh	Eugene Kinkade	New Martinsville
Eighth	Jack Kendall	Portland
Ninth	Joe Wood	Columbus GA
Tenth	Eugene Millard	Bloomington IL

The prize list was again bountiful.

First	$2,000 scholarship to any state college or university
	First-place national silver trophy
	Gold medal—Diamond set
Second	Master Deluxe Chevrolet Coach
	Second-place national silver trophy
	Silver medal—Ruby set
Third	Master Chevrolet Coach
	Third-place national silver trophy
	Bronze medal—Sapphire set
Fourth	National silver trophy
Fifth	National silver trophy

International Trophies
    First-place silver trophy
    Second-place silver trophy
    Third-place silver trophy

Special Awards
C. F. Kettering Award—Silver Trophy for Best Design
    Robert Bennett, Long Island, NY
Indianapolis Speedway Award—Fastest Heat
    Robert Ballard, White Plains, IN
Chevrolet Silver Trophy—Best Upholstery
    Billy Kindrick, Little Rock, AR
Best Brake Design
    Waldron Stemm, Schenectady, NY

Each champion received a gold Waltham wristwatch and a driver's diploma awarded by Chevrolet.

Ballard with his trophies

Sidelights, as Reported in the *Akron Beacon Journal*

For the St. Paul champ, thirteen-year-old Robert Holland, winning his local race was bittersweet. Robert, whose brother won in 1936, scored his victory unaware that his mother had passed away in the hospital after an operation. Before she lapsed into unconsciousness, she said,

"Don't tell him until after the race. He must race just the same." Before he started for Akron, he looked down at his mother's peaceful face as she lay in her coffin. "Gosh," he sobbed, "I wish that I had lost and Mother had won." Robert won his first heat in Akron but was nosed out later.

The Peoria representative, Robert Thompson, was taken to the hospital just after he won his local race with an attack of acute appendicitis. Physicians held him three days for observation and then allowed him to come to Akron before having an operation. A substitute driver accompanied Robert in case of another attack. None came, and Robert was able to win his first heat.

J. B. Houck, who won in Memphis, drove barefoot, and for good reason. He had never owned a pair of shoes. The thirteen-year-old, who was one of nine children and fatherless, had known poverty all his life. He took $6.50 of his prize money and bought a pair of shiny new shoes to wear to Akron. He was beaten in his initial heat.

Helena, Montana, champ Andy Rummel limped up to the Mayflower Hotel desk to register Wednesday night. He didn't receive the customary welcome of a blaring band. He arrived so early that he surprised everyone. Andy limped because he was the victim of infantile paralysis. He was scheduled for an operation on his twisted leg upon his return to Helena. He also lost his first-round heat.

Five times in the day's racing, the photo-finish camera was needed to determine the winner. Thirty seconds after the cars hit the finish stripe, an eight-by-ten photo was produced for the judges to view.

There was an interesting lull during the races while motion picture representatives staged a race sequence for a scene in a forthcoming movie in which Jackie Cooper was to play a derby contestant. Down the hill came Walter Aylstock of Cincinnati and Murrel Holt of Des Moines in lanes one and two. They finished in a dead heat.

Jack Wyatt, twelve, of Anderson, Indiana, had the closest call of the day. He was only a few feet from the finish line when a gangling dog trotted out into his path. *Wham!* Jack's racer bounced the dog off the track, skidded across the line, and bounced into the sideboard along the track. The car was damaged slightly, but Jack was not hurt.

Harland Forstner, also twelve, of Boise, Idaho, lost control of his speedster on the hill and failed to finish. His car turned round and round and then rolled to a stop.

Facts

Although there was a lot of swerving and creeping out of lanes, there were no penalties invoked. The rules stated that as long as there was no interference with another racer, everything was fine. While Robert Ballard veered out of his lane several times, he was always well ahead of his competition.

While the 1936 ticket was a work of art, the1937 one was generic and not worth noting. The program was an exact duplicate of the 1936 one except for the names of the contestants.

Myron Scott, the founder of the Derby, served as its general manager for 1934, 1935, and 1936. He would relinquish this position to Jack Gormley in 1937. Scottie would return in 1946 and serve again through 1954.

Through the first three years of the derby, there had never been a heat so close that a photo-finish picture was needed to determine the winner. That changed in 1937.

While no champ won his city race three years in a row, three champs won their city races in 1934 and repeated in 1935. Two won in 1934 and again in 1936, and ten won in 1935 and repeated in 1936. This all came to an abrupt end in 1937. The rules committee inserted a rule that once a city winner competed in the All-American, his racing career was over.

Bale '35   Muench '36   Ballard '37

Procedure

Since the derby was an entirely new entity, 1933 and 1934 were formative years. A lot of trial and error was involved. Mistakes were made, but lessons were learned. Since local races were run on city streets, spectators coming onto the track during the racing became a safety concern. By the third year, Derby officials recognized the need for fences. In 1935, the entire Tallmadge Hill track was fenced off, as was the newly constructed Derby Downs. While the only guardrails on city streets were the curbs, wooden two-by-tens were installed at the new track. The international championship heat was a mismatch both in 1936 and 1937, and for several more years this held true. Finally in 1946 it was discontinued, and the foreign champs were included in the regular competition.

EPILOGUE

After four years, the program was a tremendous success. The All-American Soap Box Derby was becoming an American institution. Chevrolet and the nation's newspapers had done a wonderful job of promotion, and there was no reason why it would not get bigger and better each year. The sky was the limit. Nothing short of a world war could halt its progress now.

ABOUT THE AUTHOR

Growing up in the Akron area, Ronald Reed was infected, at an early age, with what is known as Derby Fever. It is a well-known malady that affects youngsters from seven to seventy every July and August. As he puts it, "I got hooked at age seven and never recovered. There is no other sound like a derby car rolling down the track." It has been his dream to obtain a photo of every heat ever run at Derby Downs. While this might seem to be an impossible goal, don't count him out. He has amassed 73 percent of them and is still collecting. They are housed at his home in the Akron suburb of Mogadore. This collection numbers more than sixty thousand pictures and is the official archive of the Derby. In 1974, he began carving miniature replicas of the winning racers, complete in detail down to the paint, lettering, and helmet color.

Many of his creations are on display at the All-American Soap Box Derby Hall of Fame and Museum at Derby Downs. As his wife, Sandy, puts it, "With Ronnie, it's not a hobby; it's an obsession."